The Bible and Its Authority

by

I. Howard Marshall

HEADLINE SPECIAL

Published on behalf of Headway by

MOORLEY'S Print & Publishing

British Library Cataloguing in Publication Data.
A catalogue record for this book is available from the British Library.

ISBN 0 86071 541 8

MOORLEY'S Print & Publishing
23 Park Rd., Ilkeston, Derbys DE7 5DA
Tel/Fax: (0115) 932 0643

1

THE PROBLEM OF AUTHORITY

Many Christians in the UK today would express their view of the value and place of the Bible in such a phrase as: 'the divine inspiration of Holy Scripture and its consequent entire trustworthiness and supreme authority in all matters of faith and conduct' (from the Basis of Faith of the Evangelical Alliance). Others would question whether the Bible should have such a privileged place in enabling us to decide what we should believe and how we should live as Christians in the modern world. In this booklet we shall concentrate our attention on the idea of the Bible as the 'supreme authority'. What does this phrase mean? Can this understanding of the place of the Bible be defended? And how does it work out in practice?

Discussions of biblical and theological matters should begin with agreement on the definitions of what we are talking about, since careful definitions make for better thinking and may indeed solve some questions before we start. Therefore it may be helpful to start by asking what we mean by 'the Bible' and by 'authority'.

What is the Bible?

Which Bible?

It may seem that we hardly need take time to define what we mean by the word 'Bible' – or do we? Surely the Bible is the well-known collection of 66 books, available to us in a variety of translations, which constitute the literary foundation for the Christian church? Even this simple definition leaves some room for debate. The restriction of the contents of the Bible to 66 books is not accepted by two of the world's major Christian groupings, the Roman Catholic Church and the Orthodox Churches, both of which include a substantial number of other books written in the period between the completion of the Old Testament and the writing of the New Testament. This booklet does not afford the space to enumerate the good reasons why Protestant Christians hold to the shortest canon. Even if the enlarged canon were accepted, however, the effects on Christian doctrine would be pretty minor.

Which version?

Then there is the question of the many different modern translations with their varying wording. The problem is even more acute if we bring in the Authorised (King James) Version and similar versions which are based on texts in the original languages that differ in many small details from the text underlying most modern translations; in a number of cases these details may have doctrinal significance. In the early centuries of the church the variety of wording in the different manuscripts of the New Testament in Greek and other languages was even greater than that between modern translations.

There are two considerations that effectively deal with this problem. The first is that the various translations and manuscripts of the Hebrew and Greek Testaments should be assessed by their fidelity to the texts 'as originally given'. This principle recognises that there were autographs of the original books (e.g. the letter that Paul actually wrote to the Philippians) and that these constitute the final court of appeal. To be sure, there is what looks like an impenetrable barrier, namely that these hypothetical originals have perished; however, reconstructing them is a feasible task for scientific scholarship making use of the early copies which have survived.

At this point the second consideration becomes relevant, namely that the amount of significant difference between the various scholarly translations (and reconstructions of the original text) is not great and does not in any case affect the essential doctrinal teaching of the Bible. Writing at the end of last century the leading textual scholars B.F. Westcott and F. J. A. Hort asserted that if their principles were sound the amount of substantial variation could scarcely be more than a thousandth part of the entire text. A subsequent century of meticulous study has scarcely altered that verdict. We have therefore, a sound basis for our claim that we have a reliable text of the Bible.

What is in the Bible?

The Bible is a collection of books, composed of two sub-collections that were brought into being over a period of several hundred years. Within these collections there is a remarkable variety of types of material. We have some books that are essentially historical, in the sense that they purport to give accounts of actual events in history, although like all historical books what they give is an interpretation, an account of events and their significance. There are collections of discourses given by religious leaders (some 'official' and some unrecognised by authority) to the people, and these writings express what the authors believed that God wanted to say.

Some of this material claims to tell what God will do in the future and is couched as prophecy (although prophecy is far more than simply forecasting the future). There are other narratives (like the parables or stories told by Jesus) which fall more into the area of fiction in the sense that the stories are 'made up' (though some may be based ultimately on actual events and people), and they are there to teach some lesson or other. There is also a considerable amount of material describing what people have said to God (such as the Psalms) rather than what God might want to say to the people. Some of the writing is meant to be understood pretty literally, but other parts of it use all the resources of imagery to make their point, and sometimes it is not clear whether the language is straightforward or symbolical, and, if the latter, what the symbolism is meant to represent.

All of this demonstrates that the Bible is not in any simple sense 'The Word of God' as if we could read it and immediately deduce what God is saying to us. It is already becoming apparent that it is not all a repository of direct words from God to humankind; what it is saying needs interpretation, and even then we may not always be entirely sure what the original authors meant.

And finally, the Bible was written for varied audiences who lived at least two millennia ago and not directly for us. The same parent may have to say different things to different sons, telling the timid one to go ahead and take risks and telling the adventurous one to play it safe. Within the Bible itself opposite things needed to be said: Jesus had to tell people both to let their light shine so that people could see their good works and also to do their good deeds in secret lest they gained human praise. Does God have to say different things to us from what he said to past generations? How can the Bible be authoritative for today?

What is authority?

The meaning of 'authority'

The term 'authority' also needs some unpacking. It can refer to a number of different things.

First, there is the difference between supreme and delegated authority. Imagine a country with a king or dictator who has supreme, absolute power. He has no need to appeal to anybody else to justify or back up his decisions. His commands are absolute. But if his army or police force interfere in the lives of the people of the country, they do so only because they have delegated authority from the ruler to do what he commands; if they act in other ways (such as by taking bribes or killing innocent people), they are acting without authority.

Second, there is a distinction between the authority of power and the authority of knowledge. The authority of power is that possessed by the dictator who has an army and guns at his disposal to ensure that his authority is respected; take away his army, or bring a stronger force against him, and it becomes clear that his authority is simply that of force. But there is also the authority of the doctor at the scene of an accident who may tell the other people who are trying to help not to move the wounded person since (from her medical knowledge) she knows that to try to help in this way will only make things worse. Here a person speaks with authority because she has a medical training which entitles her to respect and obedience. This does not mean that her authority is absolute; we generally count the skill of the experienced consultant more highly than that of the newly graduated house doctor, and there is such a thing as a 'second opinion' on a patient. Nevertheless, the basic point is clear, namely that there is an authority which belongs to knowledge.

Third, there is a distinction between absolute and relative authority. The doctor's authority is not total. It may be based on partial knowledge, and therefore there can be room for discussion on the best diagnosis of the patient's condition and the best treatment to adopt. It may also be limited to a specific area: the doctor in question may not be an authority on cancerous diseases, still less on the best way to design a road transport system. It is, therefore, the authority of knowledge that is the real issue, rather than the authority of persons possessing knowledge, and the question then becomes one of identifying where genuine knowledge is to be found.

A further problem is of course the question whether there is such a thing as 'genuine' knowledge. Within the confines of a system of mathematical postulates and axioms there can be a limited set of absolutes, such that 3 x 3 = 9, and there can be no dispute about this whatsoever. But if it is a matter of morality or aesthetics there may be no such thing as irrefutable knowledge. The question of 'authority' then becomes all the more difficult.

We need the authority of knowledge when we ourselves lack knowledge; by definition, therefore, the person with the authority of knowledge has something that we do not have, and we are unable to check up directly on its truth and validity; instead, we have to exercise trust or faith that the authority is justified (perhaps we have other reasons for recognising their credibility, as when the person claiming medical skills is known to have graduated in medicine at a reputable medical school.) We exercise this kind of trust continually in ordinary daily life; it is built on trust that other people know what they are doing although we cannot check up for ourselves.

Different sources of authority

The authority that we ascribe to the Bible is concerned with knowledge. To be sure, power is involved. We saw that the helpers at the accident had to follow the directions of the doctor. In that the doctor has knowledge she has the power or authority to command. The dictator also had authority to command, but this rested on no better grounds than the possession of force.

The question of authority in religion is a question that relates in the first place to knowledge. It is the question of how we can know about God and his will for us as human beings. Although this is a very wide question, we can legitimately narrow it down in this booklet since we are thinking within the context of Christian belief. The question arises within a community that stretches far and wide in time and place and that has a common understanding of the nature of God, of his redemptive revelation in his Son Jesus Christ, and of his ongoing relationship with his people through his Holy Spirit. Within the church there is a common understanding that in some way the Bible is a source of knowledge about God and his will.

Within this community and this broad framework of belief we would find general agreement that there are four basic ways in which people can have knowledge of God.

First, all agree that in some sense *the Bible* mediates knowledge of him to us. It was written by people who witnessed what they believed to be a revelation by God in three areas: in the history of the Jewish people, supremely in the life, death and resurrection of Jesus and the subsequent development of the Christian church, and in their own personal religious experience. At the very least, then, the Bible contains witness to these events. But of course it is more than that. It contains the utterances of people who said 'Thus says the Lord', or who had experiences in which they believed that God (or an agent of God) spoke to them, or who felt inwardly that what they were saying was inspired by the Spirit of God or was in agreement with the mind of the Spirit.

Second, all agree that God continues to speak to his people in *the life and experience of the Christian church.* The word 'tradition' is often used to designate the collective wisdom of Christian people. It contains, for example, a broad understanding of how the Bible is to be understood and its teaching applied, and it may be a source of further understanding and fuller development of what was learned at an earlier stage. Naturally, there are traditions and traditions, some of which may be contradictory, some accepted in one part of the church and others in another. But the belief that God guides his church and gives it fresh light or specific guidance in changing circumstances is not affected by this uncertainty over what is universally acceptable truth.

Third, there is the function of what is generally called *'reason'*, by which is meant human intellectual activity of whatever kind (including both the use of senses and the use of argument) in order to arrive at new knowledge and to assess the validity of existing knowledge. The vast bulk of our knowledge about ordinary matters comes through this source. The difficult question is how far human reason has an authoritative role in relation to religion as opposed to its role in the ordinary affairs of life. Is not religion a matter primarily of revelation rather than human attempts to discover ultimate truth?

And fourth, there is the function of *personal experience*, which says that in the end we are responsible for our own decisions about what we believe and do, and that our consciences cannot be bound by any external agency. We have the right and the authority to come to our own conclusions, and we are not bound by the authority of the church or by reason – or by the Bible?

Here, then, are four different, but closely related, modes of knowledge, and most people would agree that all four are actual and necessary. The set is sometimes referred to as 'the Methodist Quadrilateral' and represents John Wesley's enlargement of the Anglican identification of 'Scripture, tradition and reason' as authorities by adding experience to the list. Different groups of people, however, may emphasise one or other of them or elevate it to a supreme position, while others may state that we cannot create a theoretical hierarchy of sources of knowledge and elevate one above the others. So the issue is not one of choosing one mode of knowledge and ignoring the others; all are needed, and the question is whether one of them stands above the others when it comes to the rub. Donald English has helpfully suggested that for some people the four modes of knowledge are like the parts of a mobile, four equal cut-outs strung out on branches suspended from the central string, but for other people one cut-out is actually on the main string and the other three revolve around it. It would appear that for John Wesley himself Scripture was his central authority, and this is certainly the view of the Deed of Union of the Methodist Church which bases 'our doctrines' on 'the divine revelation recorded in the Holy Scriptures' and holds this revelation to be 'the supreme rule of faith and practice'. Which view is right?

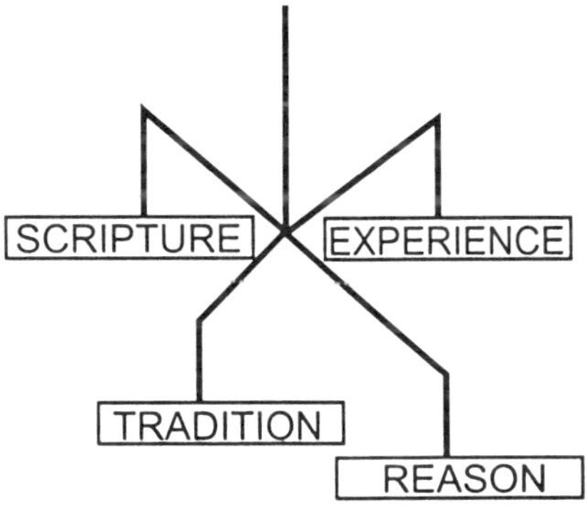

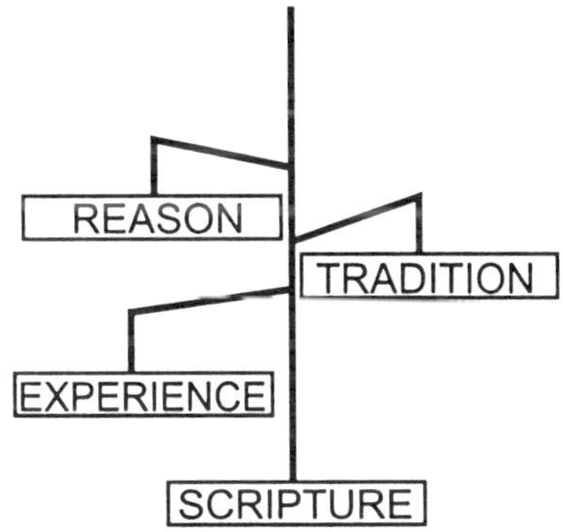

The traditional *Protestant* position, espoused by the Deed of Union, has been to regard the Bible as the supreme authority in all matters of faith and conduct. This means that where there is a dispute between what is suggested by the Bible, tradition, reason and a person's own experience, then the Bible is the arbiter and can over-rule the others.

The traditional *Roman Catholic* position, by contrast, elevates the place of the church and its traditions. Although it is careful to include the Bible as the major tradition, nevertheless in classical Catholicism the church is ultimately supreme over the Bible because it carries the authority from God to interpret it.

Within certain parts of what we may call *liberal Protestantism* it is reason which has been supreme, and the teachings of the Bible and the church have been examined, and sometimes rejected or reinterpreted, on the grounds that they are contrary to the insights of reason, as it uses both the empirical method of appealing to evidence and more abstract reasoning and cogitation.

And, finally, there is the tendency to insist that the individual's own experience is the final arbiter between the different claims to authority; ultimately it is what we ourselves believe to be right, what harmonises with our own experience that we must accept. This view is perhaps especially congenial in our own day with its 'pluralism' of beliefs, where each person is entitled to their opinions and what is true for me is not necessarily true for anybody else, and where indeed this freedom is held to be essential since there is no absolute truth for all people anyhow.

The last of these positions is currently popular under the label of *post-modernism*, although it is by no means a new position. It is open to the objection that for people to live together in community there must be some accepted common beliefs and practices (e.g. respect for persons, no murder, no rape). These principles can then be accepted simply as useful expedients without anybody necessarily arguing that they are necessarily valid for all people at all times. Nevertheless, the acceptance of them presumes some kind of belief that it is good to have a community in which people live together in peace; and once we have admitted this, we are on the road to admitting that there are some things which are universally true. From a Christian point of view it is difficult to see how the pluralist position can be justified in that, if Christianity is anything, it is a religion which accepts the centrality of Jesus and makes certain beliefs about him non-negotiable. Radical pluralism is inconsistent with Christian faith.

The claims of reason again are obviously important. But there is already so much in life which is not decided by reason, such as falling in love or likes and dislikes in music, that it is not too difficult to argue the case that there are some areas in which reason is not the supreme arbiter. The nature of Christian faith with its emphasis on truth that comes from God effectively rules out the supremacy of reason.

The case for the church and its tradition being supreme in religion and morality is stronger. It is important here that the Bible needs to be interpreted: has not God provided for its interpretation by giving the church the ability to do so, and must there not be authority in the body that makes the interpretative decisions? But then we must ask about the nature of that authority and where is it to be found? Different church bodies can claim authority over different groups of believers and even one church can change its mind over the years regarding its interpretation of the Bible. We are back with a kind of pluralism.

Is the Bible supremely authoritative?

The Bible as authoritative and inspired

Why should the Bible be regarded as supremely authoritative? Does it fare any better than the alternatives? There is the obvious fact that it is a collection of documents which are associated with the establishment of the Christian church. It includes the documents regarded as authoritative by the first Christians, and these were written by people who were among the principal characters in the early church or were able to record what happened (particularly as regards the life and teaching of Jesus). Proximity to the events is accordingly important. Any attempt to remain faithful to the origins of the church must necessarily treat the earliest documents with respect. The point can also be made that these are the only contemporary documents we have which narrate and interpret the events which were understood to be God's saving and judging interventions in human history.

However, there is considerably more to it than simply antiquity. The documents include writings by people who believed that God was conveying a revelation to them, whether directly (as in the case of the Revelation of John) or less directly in their capacity as God's agents guided by the Holy Spirit in their teaching to the churches (e.g. Paul). The content of the gospel and the instruction to Christian believers was regarded as 'the word of the Lord'. As for the Jewish Scriptures, which were accepted by Christians as their Scriptures also, two writers describe these as being 'God-breathed' or written by people 'moved by the Holy Spirit' (2 Timothy 3:16; 2 Peter 1:21). These factors combined to form the basis for a doctrine of 'inspiration', according to which the human authors were inspired by the Holy Spirit so that their writings are an expression of the 'Word of God'.

This doctrine, which was stated in 2 Timothy to be descriptive of 'all Scripture', applies to the New Testament as well as the Old Testament. It entails that the biblical writers were expressing the Word of God whether they were directly recording revelations which they had received or were themselves composing what they wrote (like Paul writing a letter or an unknown author recording the history of Israel and Judah). In some cases the writers were behaving as prophets so that what they wrote was what they believed that God was directly communicating to them. But in other cases (such as that of a historian or the writer of a psalm pouring out his soul in prayer) the writer was not the recipient of direct revelation, and 'moved by the Holy Spirit' is taken to mean that God was able to overrule what they were writing so that it expressed adequately what he wanted to be said while preserving their human integrity and individuality. J. I. Packer has popularised the term 'concursive' to express the manner in which the Holy Spirit was at work so that the humanly-written book was at the same time the expression of the Word of God. More recently, N. Wolterstorff has helpfully developed the idea of 'authorisation' to describe how God in effect has given his imprimatur to the work of the human agents, so that what they wrote now carries his authority.

The implication of this doctrine is that the Bible in its several parts is authoritative in that its writers were inspired and authorised by God and were recognised to be so by the immediately following generations of Christians – not, it should be added, without considerable debate over which books to recognise; this was no hasty, ill-thought-out decision. Since there is no other source of revelation of which this is true, it is arguably the supreme authority for our knowledge of God.

But to say that this doctrine is in fact the collective teaching of the biblical writers themselves (whether of some New Testament writers affirming that the Hebrew Bible was authoritative Scripture or of these same writers claiming in effect to stand in the same succession of writers of Scripture) is of course to recognise that it is a doctrine deduced from the documents to which it applies; and it offers us the invitation to share in their self-understanding. Acceptance of the doctrine is thus ultimately a matter for faith. We can claim that this is what the biblical writers believed about themselves and about one another. We can give good reasons for accepting their testimony, but in the end we have to decide whether or not we believe that testimony.

Problems of Biblical authority

What factors, then, influence our decision whether or not to accept it? One factor is whether this is a fair understanding of how the biblical writers understood their own role. Have we a firm exegetical basis for it? On this point the matter is reasonably straightforward. The detailed exposition of the basis for this understanding of the nature of the Bible is impressive, and the reader must be referred to fuller treatments elsewhere for substantiation of this point. B. B. Warfield was the magisterial expositor of the doctrine at the end of last century in an impressive work of scholarship. At a more popular level but in no less scholarly fashion J. I. Packer has restated the case for the contemporary reader. Together they have shown that this understanding was that of the biblical authors.

A second factor is whether the doctrine is credible. The issues that arise at this point have to do with the reliability of the Bible as a revelation of God. The term 'infallibility' is often used in this connection, carrying the implication that the teaching of the Bible as a whole about God is true and reliable. But, many people would object, is it not obvious that the Bible is untrustworthy as a whole? There are three areas of debate.

a. There is the problem of how so many different writers over so long a period of composition can have produced a unified work so that one can legitimately speak of 'what the Bible says' on any topic. How does one draw out a Christian doctrine from a set of documents which are not all in the form of actual teaching?

b. There is the problem of apparent error and contradiction on matters of historical fact and the like.

c. There is the problem of apparent error and contradiction in the area of teaching about belief and practice.

It is the difficulty felt by many people in answering these problems satisfactorily that leads them to reject the general concept of an inspired, infallible and authoritative Bible.

We must honestly admit that people who do hold this concept do so with the clear recognition that their belief entails problems to which they do not always have full answers. Nevertheless, they hold their belief because for them it is more credible than the alternatives.

a. The problem of the unity of biblical teaching is to be answered by recognising that the process of revelation has taken place over a long period as people came to a fuller understanding of God (not without some relapses on the way), and the teaching must be seen as culminating in the revelation in Jesus. This revelation includes not only the actual facts of his life and teaching but also the fuller understanding of him and his significance which came to his followers after his resurrection and the coming of the Spirit. Some parts of the Bible offer a partial understanding which can be misleading if taken on their own. There can be differences in manner of expression and content of teaching on the surface which may nevertheless be based on an underlying common understanding. Therefore, it is essential to emphasise that the authority of Scripture does not necessarily reside in individual statements taken on their own but rather in the teaching of the whole, with the individual statements being understood in the context of the Bible as a whole and seen as a testimony to God's action which is focussed in Jesus and the coming of the Spirit.

b. The primary purpose of the Bible is not to provide detailed accurate historical and geographical information, but what it does teach is adequate for God's purpose in the way in which it is given. We do not go to the Bible primarily for scientific and historical information, although it is certainly a source for some such information. In the nature of things the Bible cannot be proved to be true in all its statements (and their implications). The real issue is whether the historical problems that do arise are so many and so serious that the doctrine appears less rather than more credible.

   Obviously some historical points are of greater importance than others. If Christ did not rise from the dead, then our faith is empty and pointless. However, the authority of the Bible in doctrine and ethics is scarcely affected by many of the discussions over the historicity of the underlying material; what matters is what the text says on the theological and ethical level. The most important thing is not whether Jesus said word-for-word everything that is reported in the Gospel of John; what does matter is whether the Evangelist is truly reporting the significance of Jesus for believers and unbelievers and whether Jesus was in fact such a person as he is here signified to be. Sceptics are always going to be around finding reasons to question the basic accuracy of the information in the Bible, but there continue to be sound reasons for affirming it.

c. The real problems arise where there is apparent contradiction and unacceptability in the area of biblical teaching. Problems arise when, for example, God is presented in some parts of the Bible as behaving in ways which appear to be incompatible with his character as the Father of the Lord Jesus Christ. Some of his judgements in the Old Testament appear to be carried out by means of actions as cruel and arbitrary as those which are condemned elsewhere. And even in the New Testament there can be problem passages also. Many of us ordinary Christians simply ignore these passages; we either don't know they are there or we quietly pass by on the other side. Others argue that there were people who misunderstood God and misrepresented him, and that we must go by the mainstream; not even Paul always got it right! Neither of these approaches is satisfactory. We must find a better way:

Using the Bible as our authority

We can now set out an understanding of how the Bible functions as an authority in the following points:

1. Jesus Christ is the centre of the Christian revelation, both in his teaching and in his person and work. As the risen Lord he continues to be the mediator of God to humankind both for salvation and for the knowledge of salvation. Therefore, he is the focal point of divine authority for his people. The Bible is to be read in relationship to its centre. But it must be insisted that the only Jesus that we can know is the biblical Jesus and not any subjective ideas of our own as to what Jesus might have done or said in a given situation – it is all too easy to re-make Jesus in our own image!

2. The story that leads up to his coming is one of a people coming to a developing knowledge of God, and the revelation that they receive is sometimes limited and partial because they could not yet appreciate

the full revelation of God. Therefore, it is all the more essential that the Old Testament be read, as it were, through the eyes of Christ, that its message be mediated through him. This means that there were commands given by lawgivers and prophets that were limited in application, and it also means that the teaching can be misleading if not seen in the light of the fuller revelation.

3. The full significance of Jesus is not seen simply in the record of his earthly life; he is the risen Lord and his disciples could not fully appreciate him until after his resurrection and exaltation. Therefore we need the apostolic revelation in order to understand him and his message fully. But the apostolic witness too is given in specific situations and therefore is also partial and fragmentary. It too must be seen in relation to the focal point. Some parts of the witness are more central, others more peripheral.

4. On a superficial reading some of the witnesses may seem to clash with one another in what they say or imply. A well-known case is the way in which Paul insists on justification by faith alone, whereas James speaks of a faith that is dead without works. A deeper reading shows that both are in fundamental harmony, since Paul is concerned that his readers have a faith that works by love and James is concerned about people whose faith is a matter of mere words and not a life-changing experience. We get a fuller understanding by having this apparent tension between the two writers.

5. It follows, then, that we must read the texts not only in their immediate context to avoid misunderstanding their immediate import but also in their 'Christian' context so that we see them as parts of the total revelation given by Christ and as fitting in harmoniously with it.

6. We also have to bear in mind that we are seeking to understand and apply Scripture in an imperfect world of sinful people and it is not always possible to isolate biblical teachings, especially on behaviour, and absolutise them; principles must be taken alongside one another and this may lead to some being relativised. For example, sometimes the command to love may take priority over the command not to kill or injure, and it may be necessary to use force to restrain a wrongdoer out of love for the victim.

7. In applying Scripture to our situation today we have to discover what are the eternally valid truths and commands that are expressed in the context of a particular time and culture and then reapply them

> to the situation in which we find ourselves. The strong imperative of Jesus that disciples should wash each other's feet (John 13:14f.) made sense as an expression of humble loving service in the context of ancient Palestine but today we would have to use some other symbol to express our commitment to the fundamental principle at stake, namely humble, loving service.

Along these lines we can affirm the authority of Scripture in our Christian faith and conduct. But will it work in practice?

2

AUTHORITY IN PRACTICE

How, then, do we use the Bible? A worked example may be the best way to proceed. By seeing what we do in a typical case we can then frame a procedure to be applied more generally. I take the difficult question of divorce. How do we use and recognise the Bible as our authority in this area?

What does the Bible say?

Setting out the evidence

The first thing that we must do is to set out the evidence for the different strands of biblical teaching.

1. The Old Testament assumes the practice of divorce in its laws and merely regulates how it is practised (Deut 24:1-4).
2. The Old Testament chronicles the divorcing of foreign wives at God's command in the community that settled in Jerusalem after the exile (Ezra 9-10).
3. The prophet Malachi declares God's opposition to divorce (Mal 2:16).
4. Jesus declared that divorce and remarriage is tantamount to adultery and forbade the separation of those whom God has joined (Mark 10:1-12; cf. Matthew 19:1-12; Luke 16:18).
5. Jesus stated that divorce by a husband is adultery except where the wife has already committed adultery (Matthew 5:31f; cf. 19:9).
6. Jesus in effect pronounced (God's) forgiveness on a woman who had committed adultery while at the same time commanding her not to commit it again (John 7:53 – 8:11).
7. Paul apparently allowed separation where the non-Christian partner in a marriage wished to separate, with the possible implication that the Christian partner was then free to remarry (1 Cor 7:15).
8. Paul accepted the common view that a person is 'bound' to their spouse until the latter's death and is then free to remarry (Romans 7:2f.; 1 Corinthians 7:39).

Interpreting the evidence

We remind ourselves what we are trying to do. We have two questions to answer. Is there a biblical line on this matter so that one could (to put it rather simplistically) say 'The Bible says...'? And if we can discover what the Bible says, how do we respond to it today?

In order to deal with the first of these questions we now need to see whether the Biblical evidence can be put together in a synthesis that is coherent and does not distort or ignore any part of it.

1. There is a clear difference between the assumed practice in the OT legislation and the declaration of principle in the NT. Nevertheless, in Malachi 2:16 we have an anticipation of the NT teaching. It is arguable that in Ezra's case there was a conflict between the commands not to practise idolatry and not to break up a marriage; the former command took precedence and the dissolution of the marriages with non-Israelites was seen as the lesser evil – it being assumed that marriage to Canaanite women was a step on an inevitable path to religious apostasy (witness the influence of a Jezebel on Ahab). Paul's teaching in his situation is different from that of Ezra in that he counsels against the break-up of marriages because one partner is not a Christian. He evidently takes the more optimistic view that the Christian partner may lead the other to faith. (Peter can be assumed to hold the same view [1 Pet 3:1f.].)

2. Jesus upheld the ideal of lifelong faithfulness in marriage and based it on an interpretation of the principle in the creation story and the Creator's intention for marriage. He states that divorce followed by remarriage is sinful. To have a sexual relationship with somebody other than your married partner is to commit the sin of adultery whether it takes place while you are still married to the partner or whether you divorce him/her in order to do so. Matthew's wording could be taken to mean that if your partner has already committed adultery then in this case the marriage bond has already been severed and you are free to divorce.

3. The teaching of Jesus took place at a time when Jewish teachers had differing views on the legitimacy of divorce. One group forbade divorce to the husband except in response to adultery committed by the wife, while the other allowed it if for other reasons the wife had ceased to find favour in his eyes. At the very least Jesus sided with the former group, and, if he forbade remarriage even after adultery, he went even further than they did.

4. It is very important to note here that in the Judaism of the time of Jesus a husband's sexual relationship with a woman other than his wife was not regarded as adultery, but if a wife had relationships with a man other than her husband she was guilty of adultery against her husband. By his ruling Jesus eliminated this inequality and regarded a husband who has a sexual relationship with another woman as being just as culpable as a wife who behave similarly. Where the wife has already committed adultery, the divorce is not adultery by the husband (and vice versa).

5. But why should adultery be regarded as sinful? In some societies the wife is regarded as the possession of the husband (like his slaves or his cattle), and this ownership entitles him to exclusive sexual intimacy with her; adultery is the violation of his rights of possession (and this is why the wife has no similar rights, since she doesn't 'own' her husband in the same way). The death of the husband brings his rights to an end, and the wife is then free to remarry. The logic of this position is compatible with polygamy, where a husband may have more than one wife among his possessions, unless the (male) society forbids this since there would not be sufficient women to share among the males or since polygamy leads to rivalry and difficult domestic situations.

   Clearly this rationale will not hold for Jesus and the author of Genesis (although there were people in Old and New Testament times who upheld it). For them marriage constitutes a union between two people which has been willed by God and therefore to break it is to break what God has joined together; when we bring in the broader biblical picture of marriage, it is clear that marriage is the loving union of two partners and divorce is the tearing apart of what ought to remain united. This is a much stronger basis for affirming the indissolubility of marriage than the idea of the wife as the husband's possession.

6. What is not clear, however, is the situation after the divorce. Currently there are two conflicting interpretations. According to one interpretation, Jesus is saying that remarriage after divorce (for whatever reason) is tantamount to adultery – and therefore sinful. According to the other interpretation, remarriage after divorce is permissible in the case of the partner's adultery or in the case of an unbelieving partner's desertion. The former interpretation was very widely held in the early church and has been spiritedly defended recently by G. J. Wenham and W. E. Heth. The latter

interpretation has been widely held at least since the Reformation. The debate continues.

7. It should also be remembered that Jesus refused to condemn a woman who had committed adultery while at the same time commanding her not to commit it again. This story reminds us that the concern is not just with telling people what they ought or ought not to do but also with dealing with people who have committed adultery or divorced their partners and subsequently remarried.

It is important to note that in this section we have brought in the wider sweep of biblical teaching as the theological context in which the specific references to divorce are made, and we have also attempted to understand the historical and cultural context in which the statements were made, so that we could appreciate their original significance more accurately. In doing so we have had to take into account the work of biblical scholars, both past and present, who have light to shed on the text of the Bible.

Summing up the evidence

In the light of these considerations let me attempt a synthesis of the evidence: In the Old Testament divorce was permitted and practised, although Malachi stated that God hated it. In the New Testament Jesus recognised that divorce was allowed in the Old Testament law because of the hardness (i.e. sin) of human beings, but that God's original intention was lifelong union. He commented that divorce followed by remarriage was tantamount to adultery (whether initiated by the husband or the wife). According to one view he allowed that divorce was permissible after the adultery of the partner but that this was not grounds for remarriage, whereas according to another view he allowed remarriage in this case. Paul counselled believers to allow an unbelieving partner to separate if they so desired, but whether he implied that the believer was free to remarry in this situation is debated, just as in the case of Jesus' teaching.

Understanding and accepting the biblical teaching today

We now attempt to apply the biblical teaching to our modern situation.

Some general considerations

1. The biblical teaching will be regarded as binding only by those who accept the religious basis for it. It may express what Christians believe to be God's intention for all of humanity and not just for

Jews or Christians, but if people don't believe in God they will not feel bound to accept it (unless they have other grounds for so doing). So it is for people who accept a Judaeo-Christian pattern of morality arising out of their religious belief. Clearly it cannot be imposed by force of law (supposing that Christians were in a position to do so) in a pluralist society. However, there may be grounds for promoting and accepting it (or aspects of it) which are independent of the specifically religious basis. For example, it would be generally agreed by reasonable people that the children of a broken marriage are adversely affected by divorce, and that therefore, other things being equal, this is an argument for trying to preserve a marriage rather than allow it to break up for what may be selfish reasons. (Of course, there may be cases where a divorce would be better for the children than living with the continued bickering of their parents.)

2. The teaching rests upon a specific understanding of marriage, and therefore it does not stand on its own. This comes to sharp expression in the way in which divorce and remarriage is compared with the sin of adultery. This biblical understanding of adultery is based on a view of marriage as a personal relationship and not as the ownership of a 'possession' by the husband.

3. The consistent trend of the biblical teaching is to assume the sinfulness of adultery. Nevertheless, adultery can happen, just as murder or stealing can happen although all are equally condemned as sinful. This raises the general question of how individuals and congregations deal with those who have sinned.

Putting the matter into its modern context

We must now bring into consideration some specific aspects of our modern situation which may be relevant to the application of the biblical teaching.

1. It is now possible in this country for two people to divorce simply because there is no longer a wish for the marriage to continue without any need for one of them to prove that the other is at fault.

2. There is general agreement in society at large that when a marriage breaks down the fault is usually on both sides and not just on one (although it may well be very much more on one than on the other).

3. There is also general agreement that in cases of violent behaviour the injured partner is justified in seeking divorce.

Applying the biblical teaching

1. The understanding of marriage as something to be dissolved simply by mutual consent is to be rejected by Christians. Divorce is not a matter of convenience, just as marriage is not a casual liaison to be entered into or to be dissolved lightly.

2. The Christian understanding of humanity with its universal sinfulness leads to the conclusion that the faults are seldom only on one side, although they may be much more on one side than the other. But the implication is that Christians should be much more ready to try to deal with faults, both their own and their partner's, in order to develop a deeper and more stable relationship rather than to rush to break it up. The Christian doctrine of growth in love and holiness is highly relevant here. It is also important that we recognise the need for counselling and support for married partners experiencing difficulties, and this means a practical and costly commitment to the provision of appropriate care by trained counsellors.

3. Since the teaching of Jesus is primarily concerned with rejecting the practice of divorce for the sake of contracting another marriage to somebody more attractive, it would seem that the possibility of divorce in view of cruelty is not necessarily affected by his condemnation of it. If the principle of 'no divorce' could be set aside in order to avoid idolatry and false religion in the time of Ezra, it is equally justifiable to allow divorce if it is the only way to deal with marital cruelty. That is to say, Jesus accepted that Moses allowed divorce because of human sin, and what he stated was an ideal to be practised by his followers; but there will be occasions on which the ideal does not happen, and in such cases divorce is allowable as the lesser evil.

4. In the case of adultery committed by one partner, there is such a thing as forgiveness by the injured partner (and there are doubtless degrees of culpability in the actual sin of adultery). Reconciliation is a possibility even in this situation. But where the adulterous partner wishes to end the relationship and all attempts at reconciliation have failed, divorce may be the only solution.

5. But what about remarriage? Here there is continuing debate among equally sincere and learned Christians regarding whether Jesus permitted this or not in certain circumstances. In the context of the general character of Jesus' teaching it is probable that what he is setting forth is an ideal rather than rigid legislation, and the precision

of law is not to be expected in his teaching. If what Jesus is primarily condemning is the rejection of a spouse because somebody else is more attractive, then it may be argued that in other cases (such as that of the innocent partner in the case of adultery or the victim of cruelty or in other extenuating circumstances) remarriage is a possible option. We may simply have to recognise the existence of different attitudes among Christians on this point. This may not be a very satisfactory conclusion if we want to have precise rules about everything, but the important point is the desire to follow the teaching of the Bible and to apply it lovingly and justly to our situation.

Defining a procedure

Now it is time to reflect on what we have been doing.

1. We began by *gathering together the biblical evidence*, and we found that we needed to include not only the passages that are more specifically on the issue but also those that are less directly related to it (teaching on marriage and forgiveness).
2. We attempted to *form a synthesis* of the biblical teaching. In doing so we faced three tasks. First, it was necessary to examine the texts in their contexts so that we understood what they were originally saying rather than simply reading them superficially as if they were addressed directly to us. Second, we recognised that there was a developing revelation and that we needed to see individual texts in the light of the whole. Third, we interpreted the Bible in terms of Jesus Christ as its centre, both in his own teaching and in the significance which his first followers found in him as Saviour and Lord. Principles of belief or conduct which depend on isolated verses interpreted without reference to the love and justice of God as revealed in Christ are likely to be wrong.
3. We then proceeded to *apply the teaching* to our modern situation. We found that it raised problems because it did not deal with some of the issues that concern us, especially the issue of cruelty and other sins within marriage. We had therefore to see how the text might relate to these, and this led us to see the teaching of Jesus in a different light from our first impression of it. We have also to recognise that sometimes the teaching of Scripture is not completely unambiguous, and we may then have to take a position that we believe is consistent with Scripture while recognising that there may be scope for difference of opinion and even for change in our own

understanding. At all times we have to ensure that our application is a proper interpretation of Scripture and not an attempt to make Scripture teach something that it does not teach.

4. In some ways, therefore, our *modern situation* opened our eyes to permit a fresh application of the teaching. At the same time, we found that the biblical teaching stood in opposition to various modern attitudes and practices, and we claimed that as Christians we are bound by the biblical teaching and its implications. We had to recognise, however, that our principles are not necessarily shared by a non-Christian society and it would be wrong to force them on a pluralist society, although Christians may and should use legitimate means of persuasion to encourage society to adopt principles and practices that are in harmony with the Christian revelation. But at the same time we have to be prepared to adopt positions that are out of step with society in the light of our higher loyalty to God and his Word.
5. Finally, it should be noted that we deliberately chose a rather difficult and controversial example and went through it in some detail so that we could 'trace the working' and set out the method of approach. But fortunately not all problems are as tricky as this one, and in perhaps the majority of cases it is not too difficult to read off the biblical principles and apply them to the contemporary problem.

Conclusion

The purpose of this exercise was not primarily to frame a Christian position on divorce in the light of the biblical teaching, but to see how the Bible functions and is to be used. We brought in the contributions of other sources of knowledge, but for our ultimate guidance we sought a set of principles and practices that is in accord with the Bible.

Clearly the method is applicable to other problems. I have taken an example of human behaviour, and there are many others that might have been chosen, such as war and pacifism, debts and the payment of interest, civil obedience and disobedience. In some of these cases and especially with others, such as the medical and genetic problems that loom large at the present time, our problems are not those of the biblical writers themselves. In such cases we have to look for general biblical principles that are applicable to human behaviour and then apply these to the new problems; what we have learned from the material on divorce and how the Bible deals with this problem may well be relevant to tackling other, different problems. Inevitably there will also be a considerable input of technical knowledge so that we understand the precise issues as fully as possible.

Other questions arise with regard to matters that are more doctrinal. The way in which God exercises judgement and mercy towards those who have never heard the gospel or have followed faithfully the teaching and practices of another religion is a contemporary issue of this kind, and it is here that differences may be expected to arise between those who follow the Bible closely and those who see it as merely one religious guide among many.

For acceptance of the Bible as our supreme authority in religion and life generally does make people 'different'. On one level, there is the fact that the Bible has the capacity to change lives. Who was it who commented that studying the Bible was like working in an old house to repair the electric wires, only to find that the power had not been switched off? But on another level, the fact is that living biblically is going to be different from secular living in that different standards will be accepted in both theory and practice. Biblical Christians have to be prepared to take views that may be unpopular with the rest of society, and there may come the point when they have to say 'Here I stand; I can do no other.'

FOR FURTHER READING

W. J. Abraham, *The Divine Inspiration of Holy Scripture* (Oxford: Oxford University Press, 1981).
J. Barr, *Fundamentalism* (London: SCM Press, 1977).
K. C. Boone, *The Bible Tells Them So: The Discourse of Protestant Fundamentalism* (London: SCM Press, 1990).
D. A. Carson and J. D. Woodbridge (ed.), *Scripture and Truth* (Leicester: Inter-Varsity Press, 1983).
D. A. Carson and J. D. Woodbridge (ed.), *Hermeneutics, Authority and Canon* (Leicester:Inter-Varsity Press, 1986).
G. D. Fee and D. Stuart, *How to read the Bible for all its worth* (London: Scripture Union, 1983).
T. E. Fretheim and K. Froehlich, *The Bible as Word of God* (Minneapolis: Fortress Press, 1998).
C. F. H. Henry (ed.), *Revelation and the Bible: Contemporary Evangelical Thought* (London: Tyndale Press, 1959).
I. H. Marshall, *Biblical Inspiration* (Carlisle: Paternoster Press, 1995 reprint).
J. I. Packer. *'Fundamentalism' and the Word of God* (London: Inter-Varsity Fellowship, 1958).
J. I. Packer, *God has spoken: Revelation and the Bible* (London:Hodder and Stoughton, 1972).
B. B. Warfield, *The Inspiration and Authority of the Bible* (London: Marshall, Morgan and Scott, 1951).
J. Wenham, *Christ and the Bible* (London: Tyndale Press, 1972).
N. Wolterstorff, *Divine Discourse: Philosophical Reflections on the Claim that God Speaks* (Cambridge: Cambridge University Press, 1995).

(On the question of divorce)
R. H. Stein, 'Divorce', in J. B. Green (et al.), *Dictionary of Jesus and the Gospels* (Leicester: Inter-Varsity Press, 1992), 192-9.
G. J. Wenham and W. E. Heth, *Jesus and Divorce* (Carlisle: Paternoster, 1997).

HEADWAY

A movement of Methodists committed to prayer for revival and witness to the evangelical faith.

The aims of the movement are...

- The promotion of the renewal and revival of the work, worship, and witness of the Church, particularly within Methodism, through prayer and in the power of the Holy Spirit.
- The encouragement of prayer for revival at a personal level, and in the church at home and overseas.
- The furtherance of informed theological discussion in the Church.
- The furtherance of thinking and action on ethical and social issues in a responsible and compassionate way, based on the belief that the righteous will of God must be expressed in the life of Society.
- The promotion of joint action with evangelical Christians in all denominations of the Church in local and national events.
- The promotion of mature Christian spirituality in the lives of all members of the Church.

Our basis of faith is that of the Evangelical Alliance, with a specific commitment to the Methodist understanding of salvation, as set out in the FOUR ALLS.

- All people need to be saved
- All people can be saved
- All people can know themselves to be saved
- All people can be saved to the uttermost

Membership of HEADWAY is open to any member of the Methodist Church who is in sympathy with the aims and basis of the movement. Associate membership is open to those who are not members of the Methodist Church. Further information from the Membership Secretary

Mr Neil Baldock
1 Garraways
Woodshaw
Wootton Bassett
Swindon
Wilts SN4 8LT